생활 속의 참선수행 Practice In Daily Life ⑨

One With The Universe

한마음 한뜻이 되어

한마음 한뜻이 되어
대행큰스님 법문
생활 속의 참선수행 ⑨ / 한영합본

발행일	2014년 9월 초판
영문번역	한마음국제문화원
표지디자인	박수연
편집	한마음국제문화원
발행	한마음출판사
출판등록	384-2000-000010
전화	031-470-3175
팩스	031-470-3209
이메일	onemind@hanmaum.org

ⓒ 2014(재)한마음선원
본 출판물은 저작권법에 의하여 보호를 받는 저작물이므로
무단 복제와 무단 전재를 할 수 없습니다.

One With The Universe
Practice in Daily Life ⑨
Dharma Talks by Seon Master Daehaeng

First Edition Printed September 2014
English Translation by
Hanmaum International Culture Institute
Edited by Hanmaum International Culture Institute
Cover Design by Su Yeon Park
Published by Hanmaum Publications

ⓒ 2014 Hanmaum Seonwon Foundation
All rights reserved, including the right to reproduce
this work in any form.

Printed in the Republic of Korea

ISBN 978-89-91857-32-2 (04220) / 978-89-951830-0-7 (set)

국립중앙도서관 출판예정도서목록(CIP)

한마음 한뜻이 되어 = One With The Universe : 한영합본 / 대행큰스님 법문 ; 영문번역: 한마음국제문화원. -- [안양] : 한마음출판사, 2014
  p. ;   cm. -- (생활 속의 참선수행 = Practice in daily life ; 9)

한영대역본임
ISBN 978-89-91857-32-2 04220 : ₩6000
ISBN 978-89-951830-0-7 (세트) 04220

설법[說法]
법문(불경)[法文]

225.2-KDC5
001.01 DDC01   CIP2014026232

One With The Universe

Seon Master Daehaeng

대행큰스님 법문

차 례

- **12** 머리글
- **14** 대행큰스님에 대하여
- **22** 한마음 한뜻이 되어

Contents

- **13** Foreword
- **15** About Daehaeng Kun Sunim
- **23** One With The Universe

둘 아닌 도리

산은 물을 안고
온갖 중생 다 안고서
꽃과 나비 얼싸안고
춤을 추며 이어가네.
깊은 물은 온갖 보배
끊임없이 간직하여
한마음의 근본따라
오고 감이 전혀 없이
물바깥을 왕래하며
주해신을 본받아서
물같이 여여하게
평등공법 살라하네.

Sharing the Same Mind and Body

Mountains embrace the water,
along with all sentient beings.
Flowers and butterflies
embrace each other,
dancing and dancing.
The mountains whisper to us:
Deep waters have within them
every kind of treasure.
One mind, our foundation is the guide they always follow,
and leaving no trace of their passage,
they ceaselessly go back and forth into the world.
Grasp this essence,
live freely,
release everything into this flowing emptiness,
and live like water.

물은 산을 안고
온갖 중생 다 안고서
꽃과 나비 어우러져
꽃이 피고 열매되네.
제 나무는 제 뿌리를
간직하여 믿는다면
제 나무에 익은 열매
가고 옴이 전혀 없이
산바깥을 왕래하며
주산신을 본받아서
산같이 여여하게
평등공법 살라하네.

-대행큰스님 게송 중에서

Water embraces the mountains,

along with all sentient beings.

Flowers and butterflies

together cause blossoms to become fruit.

Water whispers to us:

When a tree cherishes its root,

relies upon its root,

the fruit that ripens on this tree

can freely go back and forth

from the mountains to the world,

with no coming or going.

Grasp this essence,

live freely,

release everything into this living emptiness,

and live like the mountains.

— Daehaeng Kun Sunim

머리글

대행큰스님이 지난 50여년 동안 끊임없이 중생들에게 베풀어주신 수많은 법문이 있었지만, 핵심을 짚어내는 하나의 단어가 있다면, 그건 아마도 "참나"일 것입니다. 항상 나와 함께 있어서 보지 못하는 내 안의 진짜 나, 그 "참나"를 발견하여 당당하고 싱그럽게 살아가기를 바라는, 중생을 위한 스님의 간절한 바램은 이 한 편의 법문 속에도 여지 없이 드러나 있습니다.

누구에게나 내면에는 만물만생을 다 먹여 살리고도 되남는 마음 속 한 점의 불씨가 있습니다. 그 영원한 불씨를 찾아 광대무변한 마음법의 이치를 체득하여, 진정한 자유인으로서, 우주의 한 일원으로서 당당히 그 역할을 해나가길 바라는 대행큰스님의 간곡한 뜻이 이 법문을 통해 여러분 모두의 마음에 전해지길 바랍니다.

한마음국제문화원 일동 합장

Foreword

Over the last fifty years, Daehaeng Kun Sunim has given countless Dharma talks and teachings to beings without number, but if all those talks could be summed up into one word, it would be "true self."

This true essence has always been with us, yet remains unseen. Discover it for yourself, and in doing so, learn to live with courage, dignity, and joy. That all beings should awaken to this true essence is Daehaeng Kun Sunim's deepest wish. When you've tasted the purest and most refreshing spring water imaginable, you naturally want to share it with others.

Within us all is this seed, this spark that feeds and sustains each and every being. Discover this eternal spark and realize its profound and unlimited ability. If you can do this, you'll know what it means to truly be a free person, and you can fulfill the great role that is yours as a member of the whole universe.

With palms together,
The Hanmaum International Culture Institute

대행큰스님에 대하여

대행큰스님은 여러 면에서 매우 보기 드문 선사(禪師)셨다. 무엇보다 선사라면 당연히 비구 스님을 떠올리는 전통 속에서 여성으로서 선사가 되었으며, 비구 스님들을 제자로 두었던 유일한 비구니 스님이었고, 노년층 여성이 주된 신도계층을 이루었던 한국 불교에 젊은 세대의 청장년층 남녀들을 대거 참여하게 만들어 한국불교에 새로운 풍격(風格)을 일으키는데 일조한 큰 스승이셨다. 또한 어느 누구나 마음수행을 통해 깨달을 수 있음을 강조하며 전통적인 수행 모델과는 달리 삭발제자와 유발제자를 가리지 않고 법을 구하는 이들에게는 모두 똑같이 가르침을 주셨고, 전통 비구니 강원과 비구니 종단에 대한 지속적인 지원을 펼치심으로써 비구니 승단을 발전시키는데 중추적인 역할을 하셨다

About Daehaeng Kun Sunim

Daehaeng *Kun Sunim*[1] (1927-2012) was a rare teacher in Korea: a female *Seon(Zen)*[2] master, a nun whose students included monks as well as nuns, and a teacher who helped revitalize Korean Buddhism by dramatically increasing the participation of young people and men. She broke out of traditional models of spiritual practice to teach in such a way that allowed anyone to practice and awaken, making laypeople a particular focus of her efforts. At the same time, she was a major force for the advancement of *Bhikkunis*,[3] heavily supporting traditional nuns' colleges as well as the modern Bhikkuni Council of Korea.

---

1. Sunim / Kun Sunim: Sunim is the respectful title of address for a Buddhist monk or nun in Korea, and Kun Sunim is the title given to outstanding nuns or monks.

2. Seon (Chan, Zen)**:** Seon describes the unshakeable state where one has firm faith in their inherent foundation, their Buddha-nature, and so returns everything they encounter back to this fundamental mind. It also means letting go of "I," "me," and "mine" throughout one's daily life.

3. Bhikkunis: Female sunims who are fully ordained are called Bhikkuni(比丘尼) sunims, while male sunims who are fully ordained are called Bhikku(比丘) sunims. This can also be a polite way of indicating male or female sunims.

대행스님은 1927년 서울에서 태어나 일찍이 9세경에 자성을 밝히시고, 일제 강점기와 6.25 전쟁을 거치면서 당신이 증득(證得)하신 바를 완성하기 위해 오랫동안 산중에서 수행하셨다. 1950년대 말경, 치악산 상원사 근처에 있는 한 움막에 머무르시며 찾아오는 수많은 사람들의 고통스런 호소를 들으시고 그들을 도와주셨다. 중생들이 가지고 오는 어떠한 문제도, 어떠한 어려운 상황도 해결이 되도록 도와주신 대행스님의 자비의 원력은 당시에 이미 한국에서는 전설이 되어 있었다. 스님은 자비를 물 마른 웅덩이에서 죽어가는 물고기를 살리는 방생에 비유하셨다. 그래서 집세가 없어 셋집에서 쫓겨난 사람들에게 집을 마련해 주고, 학비가 없어서 학교를 마칠 수 없는 학생들에게 학비를 대주셨지만, 스님의 자비행(慈悲行)을 아는 사람은 거의 없을 정도였다.

그러나, 문제를 해결해 주면 그때뿐 또 다른 문제가 닥쳐오면 속수무책이 되어 버리고 마는 사람들을 보며, 스님께서는 중생들이 자신들의 문제를 스스로 해결하고, 나아가 인과(因果)와 윤회(輪廻)[1]의 굴레에서 벗어나 자유인이 될 수 있는 도리를 가르치는 것이 더 시급하다는 생각을 하게 되었다.

Born in Seoul, Korea, she awakened when she was around eight years old and spent the years that followed learning to put her understanding into practice. For years, she wandered the mountains of Korea, wearing ragged clothes and eating only what was at hand. Later, she explained that she hadn't been pursuing some type of asceticism; rather, she was just completely absorbed in entrusting everything to her fundamental Buddha[4] essence and observing how that affected her life.

Those years profoundly shaped Kun Sunim's later teaching style; she intimately knew the great potential, energy, and wisdom inherent within each of us, and recognized that most of the people she encountered suffered because they didn't realize this about themselves. Seeing clearly the great light in every individual, she taught people to rely upon this inherent foundation, and refused to teach anything that distracted from this most important truth.

Her deep compassion made her a legend in Korea long before she formally started teaching.

---

4. Buddha: In this text, "Buddha" and "Bodhisattva" are capitalized out of respect, because these represent the essence and function of the enlightened mind. "The Buddha" always refers to Shakyamuni Buddha.

마침내 산에서 내려온 스님께서는 1972년 경기도 안양에 한마음선원을 설립하셨고, 이후 40여 년 동안 한마음선원에 주석하시며, 크고 작은 법회에서 질문을 해오는 사람들에게 그들의 근기와 여건에 맞추어 답을 해주시며 불법의 진리를 가르쳐 주셨다. 스님은 여러 다양한 사회복지 프로그램을 후원하셨고, 6개국에 10개의 해외지원과 한국 국내에 15개 지원을 세우셨으며, 스님의 가르침은 영어, 독어, 스페인어, 러시아어, 중국어, 일본어, 불어, 이태리어, 베트남어, 인도네시아어, 아랍어 등으로 번역 출간되었다. 2012년 5월 22일 영시, 세납 86세로 입적하셨으며, 법랍 63세였다.

---

1. 윤회(輪廻): 산스크리트어의 삼사라(samsara)를 번역한 말로 쉼 없이 돈다는 생사의 바퀴를 뜻함. 다시 말해, 수레바퀴가 끊임없이 구르는 것과 같이, 중생이 번뇌와 업에 의하여 삼계(三界: 색계, 욕계, 무색계) 육도(六道: 지옥, 아귀, 축생, 아수라, 인간, 천상)라는 생사의 세계를 그치지 않고 돌고 도는 현상을 일컬음.

She was known for having the spiritual power to help people in all circumstances and with every kind of problem. She compared compassion to freeing a fish from a drying puddle, putting a homeless family into a home, or providing the school fees that would allow a student to finish high school. And when she did things like this, and much more, few knew that she was behind it.

Kun Sunim saw that for people to live freely and go forward in the world as a blessing to all around them, they needed to know about this bright essence that is within each of us. To help people discover this for themselves, she founded the first *Hanmaum*[5] Seon Center in 1972. For the next forty years she gave wisdom to those who needed wisdom, food and money to those who were poor and hungry, and compassion to those who were hurting.

---

5. Hanmaum[han-ma-um]: "Han" means one, great, and combined, while "maum" means mind, as well as heart, and together they mean everything combined and connected as one. What is called "Hanmaum" is intangible, unseen, and transcends time and space. It has no beginning or end, and is sometimes called our fundamental mind. It also means the mind of all beings and everything in the universe connected and working together as one. In English, we usually translate this as "one mind."

본 저서는 대행큰스님의 법문을
한국어와 영어 합본 시리즈로 출간하는
〈생활 속의 참선 수행〉시리즈 제9권으로써
1996년 11월 3일 법형제 법회 때 설하신 내용을
재편집한 것입니다.

This Dharma talk was given by
Daehaeng Kun Sunim on Sunday, November 3, 1996.
This is Volume 9 in the ongoing series,
Practice in Daily Life.

Daehaeng Kun Sunim founded ten overseas branches of Hanmaum Seon Center, and her teachings have been translated into twelve different languages to date: English, German, Russian, Chinese, French, Spanish, Indonesian, Italian, Japanese, Vietnamese, Estonian, and Arabic, in addition to the original Korean. For more information about these or the overseas centers, please see the back of this book.

한마음 한뜻이 되어

1996년 11월 3일

　그동안 여러분과 만날 기회가 없었네요. 인사가 늦었습니다. 지난 9월 서울 대법회 때 너무들 애 쓰셔서, 정말이지 감사한 마음을 말로는 어떻게 다 표현할 수가 없습니다. 신도회장님 이하 여러분 모두 다 너무나 감사합니다.
　아직까지도 많이들 피곤하실 텐데 정신력으로 여기 이렇게 몸을 끌고 오셨네요. 제가 겪어봐도 그래요. 이번에 제가 법회 때문에 독일에 갔다가 쉬지 못하고 바로 또 캐나다를 갔었는데 너무 피곤하니까 멍멍해지는 거예요. 한국에 돌아와서 드러누웠다 일어나니까 방문이 어딘지 분간이 안 갈 정도로 그렇게 멍해지더군요. 그래서 내가 웃으면서 그랬어요. '하하, 이 정신력이 없으면 사람은 그냥 송장이구나!' 정신이 빠지면 몸은 그거 아무것도 아니에요.

One With The Universe

November 3, 1996

I'd like to thank everyone for working so hard to make the Dharma talk at the Olympic Stadium in Seoul such a success. I've been away overseas, so I'm late saying this; nonetheless, thank you. Words fail to express how grateful I feel to you.

I suspect that some of you still haven't recovered yet. You dragged yourselves here through force of will alone. This consciousness we have is so important; without it our body is just a corpse. Shortly after the Seoul Dharma talk, I went to Germany to give a series of talks, and then went straight to Canada for the opening of the new Toronto center. I was so tired I didn't know what country I was in! After returning to Korea, I woke up during the night and couldn't even find the door in my own room! I laughed

그런데 여러분, 궁금하지 않으세요? 저 스님은 왜 저렇게 지원을 여러 군데다가 내고 돌아다니는지, 또 말끝마다 왜 저렇게 주인공(主人空)[2]하면서 마음[3]을 찾으라고 간곡히 그러는지 궁금하지 않으세요? 내가 그러는 이유는 산 사람이나 죽은 사람이나 다 함께 한마음[4]으로 지구를 보존해야 우리가 살 수 있기 때문입니다. 지원을 각처에 손 닿는 데마다 내는 것은 그 지역에서 역사적 사건으로 죽은 모든 사람들, 갇혀

---

2. 주인공(主人空): 우리 모두 스스로 갖추어 가지고 있는 근본마음으로 일체 만물만생의 근본과 직결된 자리. 나를 존재하게 하고, 나를 움직이게 하며, 내 모든 것을 관장하는 참 주인이므로 주인(主人)이며, 매 순간 쉴 사이 없이 변하고 돌아가 고정된 실체가 없으므로 비어 있다고 할 수 있기 때문에 빌 공(空)자를 써서, 주인공(主人空)이라 함.

3. 마음(心): 단순히 두뇌를 통한 정신활동이나 지성을 일컫는 말이 아니라, 만물만생이 지니고 있으며, 일체만법을 움직이게 하는 천지의 근본을 뜻함. '안에 있다, 밖에 있다' 혹은, '이거다 저거다'라고 말할 수 없으며 시작과 끝이 없고 사라질 수도 파괴될 수도 없음. 시공을 초월하여 존재함.

4. 한마음: '한'이란 광대무변함, 일체가 하나로 합쳐진 것을 뜻하며, 한마음이란 만질 수도 없고 보이지도 않으며, 시공간을 초월하여, 시작도 끝도 없는 근본마음을 말함. 또한, 만물만생의 마음이 삼천대천세계와 서로 연결되어 하나로 돌아가는 것을 의미하기도 함. 다시 말해서, 한마음은 우주 전체와 그 속에서 살고 있는 일체 생명들이 근본을 통해 서로 연결되어 그 마음들이 하나로 돌아가는 모든 작용을 포함하고 있음.

after I'd woken up a bit – without this mind[6] of ours, the body just stumbles around like a robot.

If you understand this, then you probably have a good idea why I've opened so many branches, and why I'm always imploring you to discover this fundamental mind of yours, what I sometimes call *Juingong*.[7] If humanity is going to survive, both living beings as well as the dead need to become one mind and work together to preserve the Earth.

I've gone around opening centers all over the world in order to help free the consciousnesses that are trapped in that region. There are often many who died in wars and disasters, who, at

---

6. Mind(心)(Kor. –maum): In Mahayana Buddhism, "mind" refers to this fundamental mind, and almost never means the brain or intellect. It is intangible, beyond space and time, and has no beginning or end. It is the source of everything, and everyone is endowed with it.

7. Juingong [ju-in-gong](主人空): "Juin(主人)" means the true doer or the master, and "gong(空)" means empty. Thus Juingong is our true nature, our true essence, the master within that is always changing and manifesting, without a fixed form or shape. Daehaeng Kun Sunim has compared Juingong to the root of the tree. Our bodies and consciousness are like the branches and leaves, but it is the root that is the source of the tree, and it is the unseen root that sustains the visible tree.

있는 모든 영혼들에게 문을 열어 주어 한마음으로 귀정 짓게 하고, 또 산 사람들 역시 한마음이 되게 하려는 겁니다. 꼭 신도들이 아니더라도 인연이 되는 사람들과 함께 우리가 그 지역에 지원을 내기만 해도 벌써 그것은 우주하고도 직결이 되거든요. 물론 우리가 그렇게 하고 싶다고 해서 다 되는 건 아닙니다.

그래서 항상 진실한 실천이 도(道)라고 하는 겁니다. 실천하지 않는다면 맹세코 도가 아닙니다. 예를 들어, 많은 예언자들이 '물난리가 나서 사람들이 다 죽는다.'고 말은 하는데 그걸 막지는 못합니다. 그래서 예언자는 소인이라고 했던 겁니다. 저는 지금 모든 지역에서, 여기 본원에서 멀고 가까움이 없이, 전 세계의 잠자고 있는 모든 사람들을 깨우고, 갇혀 있는 사람들의 문을 열어주고, 그렇게 해서 모두가 한마음으로 이어져 보살(菩薩)[5]의 행을 하는 일꾼이 되기를 바라는 것입니다.

---

5. 보살(菩薩): 위로는 불법을 닦아 깨달음의 지혜를 얻고, 아래로는 중생을 구제하며 그들이 스스로 깨닫도록 도와주는 부처의 화현.

the moment of their death, became stuck in that place. Thus, we work to open the door for them to become one mind. Likewise, there are many living people who are similarly stuck in their thoughts, and who can become free by becoming one mind. Although it's not easy to do, when we set up a center, it becomes one with the functioning of the universe,[8] and is directly connected to everything in it.

Sincere application is the path. Truly and sincerely putting what you know into practice is the Way! Without application, there is no path forward. Knowing isn't enough. Prophets and psychics are called small people because they can only tell you what will happen, but they can't do anything about it. However, here at our Anyang center and in centers around the world, we are working to wake up those who are asleep, and to free those who are trapped. In this way, I hope that everyone here can learn to work together as one mind, and go forward in the world using your practice to help people.

---

8. This includes all visible realms, as well as unseen realms, and the principles by which they function.

그래서 저는 오늘도 이렇게 여러분과 더불어 같이 하면서 이 말을 또 합니다. "일거수일투족 주인공 당신이 하는 거니까 바깥으로 찾지 말고 꼭 안으로 찾아라. 그런데 이 언덕 저 언덕이 따로 있는 게 아니다. 우리가 정신계와 물질계가 둘이 아니게 돌아가고 있다는 사실을 알아야 한다."고 말입니다. 어디 육신과 정신이 따로따로 놉니까? 단지 여러분을 가르치기 위해서 이 언덕에서 저 언덕으로 빨리빨리 넘어서라고 하는 겁니다. 이 언덕은 물질계고 저 언덕은 정신계인데, 정신계에 도달하게 되면 물질계와 정신계가 둘 아닌 도리를 알게 됩니다. 그래서 얼른 깨달아 저 언덕으로 넘어서라고 하는 겁니다.

So, when we gather together, I'm always telling you to focus within instead of looking around outside of yourself, for every single thing is already being done by your true nature, your Juingong. If you look at the hills, no matter how far apart, they are all still connected, aren't they? Likewise, you must realize that the material realm and the unseen realm are always functioning as one. They're not separate. Do your consciousness and flesh function apart from each other? No, of course not. It's only for the sake of getting people moving that I say things like "Hurry and leave this hill and go to that hill." Here, this hill is the material realm, and that hill is the unseen or spiritual realm. If you realize the spiritual realm, you will instantly understand how it works together as one with the material realm. So I say to you, hurry up and awaken, and cross over to that hill.

As you practice trying to let your Juingong come forward, everything will begin to communicate through it. However, if you are only looking for and following the material aspects, then you won't be able to communicate or become one mind with everything. Thus, nothing you do

그 과정에서 우리가 내 근본인 주인공을 찾다 보면 거기에 모든 것이 통신이 됩니다. 그러나 물질계로만 들어간다면 통신이 되질 않아 한마음이 될 수가 없으니 공덕(功德)[6]이 될 수 없다는 사실입니다. 내 몸 안에 있는 하나 하나의 개체가 한마음이 되어 전부 따라 준다면 이게 보살의 행을 할 수 있는 공덕이 되지만 개개인으로 논다면 그렇게 될 수가 없죠. 한 회사의 직원들이 한마음이 돼서 회사를 꾸려 나간다면 회사와 직원 모두가 잘 될 뿐만 아니라 사회 다른 곳으로도 좋은 영향을 끼칠 수 있겠지만, 제가끔 논다면 잘 될 수 없는 것처럼 말입니다. 그렇기 때문에 일체 제불과 더불어 우리 모두가 한마음이 되어 이 지구를 보존해야 하는데 이렇게 마음을 합쳐서 가게 할 수 있는 도량이 있으면 좋겠다 이 말입니다.

---

6. 공덕(功德): 이 책에서의 의미는 다른 사람이나 대상을 나와 둘로 보지 않고 '내가 했다.'는 생각을 하지 않으며 조건 없이 도와주는 상태, 혹은 그렇게 함으로써 나오는 결과를 뜻함. '함이 없이 하는 것' 즉, '내가 이러이러한 일을 했다.'는 생각을 놓아버리고 해야 공덕이 됨. 아무런 조건 없이 하는 행(行)이라야만 만물만생에게 이익이 될 수 있음.

will be able to give forth true *virtue and merit*.[9] If even just the cells of your body become one mind and work together, this will give rise to the virtue and merit that will allow you to fulfill the role of a Bodhisattva.

However, if those cells argue among themselves and each goes its own way, before long the whole will break down. It's the same for companies and organizations. If everyone in a company cooperates and works together harmoniously, it will do well. Yet if everyone is arguing and fighting, it won't have much of a future. Therefore, I think it's essential that there are places dedicated to spiritual practice, where everyone can work on becoming one mind with all Buddhas and the universe, and so be able to sustain and protect the Earth.

If the Earth's air heats up, the pressure will eventually cause holes to form in the weaker parts

---

9. Virtue and merit(功德**):** Here this term refers to the results of helping people or beings unconditionally and non-dually, without any thought of self or other. It becomes virtue and merit when you "do without doing," that is, doing something without the thought that "I did such and such." Because it is done unconditionally, all beings benefit from it.

지구의 공기가 너무 더워지면 우리의 공기막은 터지게 돼 있습니다. 또 남극과 북극에 있는 빙하와 여름에도 녹지 않던 만년설이 급격히 녹게 됩니다. 그렇게 되면 이 지구에 어떤 변화가 오겠습니까? 풍비박산이 납니다. 그러면 우리는 개미떼처럼 어디 물 없는 데로 기어 올라가야 할까요? 이런 얘기는 이미 많이 들은 얘기라 안 해도 되지만 여러분이 제가 왜 이러는지 그것쯤은 조금 알고 가셔야 될 것 같아서 오늘 말합니다.

우리가 지금 공부하는 건 장난으로 하는 게 아닙니다. 종교를 믿는답시고 절이나 하고 다니는 노라리가 아닙니다. 만약 그렇게 하신다면, 더불어 같이 둘이 아닌 내 생명, 내 모습, 모두가 산산조각이 나는 겁니다. 과거에는 물에 죽고 불에 죽고 종교싸움으로 죽고 이렇게 해서 역사가 이루어졌지만 지금은 굳이 이런 천지개벽을 겪지 않고도 달라질 수 있습니다. 여러분의 마음에 달렸다는 얘깁니다.

of the atmosphere. If this happens, ice that has remained frozen for thousands of years will begin to melt too fast, and everything will change. It would be as if our entire world was torn apart. Would we be like ants fleeing a flood, struggling and climbing to find high ground? I'm bringing this up now so that you'll have some idea why I've been traveling so much and giving Dharma talks everywhere.

What I'm telling you today about relying upon your fundamental mind is desperately serious. I'm not joking around. If your idea of spiritual practice is going around visiting temples like a tourist, maybe bowing a few times in this hall or that shrine, then everything you are one with — your body, your family, your nation — will be torn to pieces. It's not an exaggeration to say that everything that exists now will be turned under the earth, so that a new era can start. In the past, the world changed only through floods, fire, wars, and the deaths of uncountable people. But now we can use our minds to change things, without having to go through these kinds of disasters. Everything changes according to how you use your mind.

이번에 독일에 가 보니까 종교싸움으로 사람들이 수없이 죽었더군요. 그래서 나는 죽을 둥 살 둥 이리저리 다니면서 죽은 사람 산 사람, 모두 각자의 생각에 갇혀 헤어나오지 못하는 사람들과 대화를 하면서, 나올 수 있는 이치를, 문을 틔워놨습니다. 그 중에는 고문당하다 죽은 수녀나 신부님들도 계셨습니다.

　우리가 이 말을 하기 전에 먼저 이야기할 게 있습니다. 사람들이 종종 "조상들을 천도(薦度)[7]시키는데 어떠한 관계로 스님께서는 우주떡 하나를 놓고 하십니까?"라는 질문을 합니다. 그렇게 하는 데는 이런 경우가 있어서입니다. 우리가 이 세상에서 극난하게 먹고 살던 관습이 남아, 죽어서도 그 관습을 떼어 버릴 수가 없습니다. 그러한 습(習)[8] 때문에, 죽어서도 살기 위해 먹으려는 그 습 때문에 자식들이나 친척한테

---

7. **천도(薦度)**: 사후에 영혼이 가야 할 길을 그 영혼의 차원대로 제대로 갈 수 있도록 인도하여 주는 깃. 일반적으로 불교의식으로 행해지는 천도재는 주로 독경, 시식, 불공 등을 베풀어 망자의 길을 인도하여 줌.

8. **습(習)**: 현재뿐만 아니라 과거 수 억겁 년 동안 행하였던 모든 행위들(말, 행동, 생각 등)이 버릇이 되어 잠재여력으로 남아 있는 것을 말함.

While visiting Germany recently, I realized that huge numbers of people had died there in religious wars. Even though I was already exhausted, I continued to go from place to place, talking with both the dead who were still trapped by the events of four hundred years ago, and the living that were trapped by their own thoughts. I told them how they could be free, and cracked open the door that had imprisoned them. Among the dead stuck in those places were many nuns and priests who had been tortured to death.

I'll come back to this story in a minute, but first let me talk about something else. Someone asked why, when holding a *cheondo*[10] ceremony we set out a plate of steamed rice cake. It's because while living in this world, the *habit*[11] of

---

10. Cheondo(薦度)**:** This involves helping the consciousness of the dead to move forward on their own path. It can happen that beings become "stuck" in their fears, attachments, and illusions, etc., and so can't move forward. Cheondo often involves a special ceremony, but not necessarily, which in a sense educates the consciousness, and so allows it to move forward at a level that more accurately reflects the level they achieved while alive.

11. Habit(習)**:** This includes not just the ways of thought and behavior learned in this life, but also all of those tendencies of thought and behavior that have accumulated over endless eons.

그냥 두더기처럼 붙어서 자기 갈 길을 가지 못하고 헤매고 돕니다. 그러면 그게 지금 산사람들뿐만 아니라 나중에 후손들에게까지도 해를 끼치게 됩니다.

　또, 많은 사찰에서 위패를 만들어 붙여놓고 법당에 오랫동안 모시는데 나는 '백일만 앉을 자릴 해놓고, 법(法)으로 설득을 해서 구원을 하라.'는 부처님의 말씀을 따르는 겁니다. 여기서 백일이란 우리 세상으로 보면 교육기간 같은 건데, 이렇게 영가들을 법당에 모셔놓고 듣게끔 하고 보게끔 해서 교육을 시켜 보내는 겁니다. 그런데 백일 동안 붙여 놓는 그 위패 때문에 때로는 영(靈)들이 갇혀 있을 수도 있습니다. 허락을 받아야 나갈 수 있으니 그 영령들은 도무지 헤어날 수가 없는 것이, 산사람으로 하여금 또 진퇴를 받아야 하는 셈이 된 겁니다. 그렇기 때문에 돌아가시면 위패를 해 놨다가 때로는 백일이 안돼도 살라 버리고 다시금 위패를 해서 영령을 모시기도 합니다. 그 이유에 대해서는 여러분이 한번 깊이 생각을 하셔야 됩니다.

eating becomes so deeply ingrained within us that many people can't set it aside even after they're dead. Because of this idea that they need food to survive, spirits often end up staying very close to their children or relatives. Thus, they cannot move forward on their own path, and in their confused state, they often inadvertently cause harm to their families and descendants.

Many other temples write the names of the deceased on a memorial paper and hang them in the Dharma Hall, but we don't do that here. Instead, we explain the Dharma to the deceased for a hundred days, so that they can move forward. Basically, this is extra time for education, where we are inviting them to see, hear, and experience this truth of one mind.

However, if you write their name on a piece of paper and leave it in the Dharma hall, that can actually hold those spirits there. To put it plainly, they now have to receive permission from the living in order to move forward, on top of the permission they need from the unseen realms. This is why when we have a ceremony for someone who has passed on, we write the memorial paper for them only on that day, and then burn it after the

그런데 어떤 경우, 사는 게 너무 힘들어 100일 동안 영가를 모셔놓고 재(齋)를 올리기 힘든 자손들은 그 영가들을 49일만 되어도 100일을 채워 보내는 천가를 하기도 합니다. 그리고 때에 따라 가난한 집의 그 조상들이 천차만별의 직책을 받아 나올 수 있도록 돕기도 합니다. 다시금 이쪽으로 태어나게 해서 선지식(善知識)[9]이 되게끔 이끌어 주면서 한편으로는 그 자손들을 위해 보살의 심부름꾼으로 일하게 하는 거죠. 이렇게 함으로써 자손들이 그 대(代)에, 그 차원의 종자가 점점점점 커지게 돼죠. 머리 깎고 중만 되는 게 선지식이 아닙니다.

---

9. 선지식(善知識): 불법의 진리를 가르쳐 주며, 사람들을 바른 길로 이끌어주는 훌륭한 지도자 혹은 현자(賢者)를 뜻함.

ceremony. If we need to have another ceremony for them later, then we write a new memorial paper for them at that time. Everyone should think deeply about why we do this.

In cases where families don't have the money for the traditional one hundred day ceremony, we tell them to hold just the forty-ninth day ceremony, and we take care of all the necessary education in that time. Also, when families are poor, I'll sometimes direct the deceased to various jobs and assignments that can help them be reborn in this world as a great being, as someone who can truly practice. As they use their practice to help others, the light of that also helps everyone who has *karmic affinity*[12] with them, including their family from their past life. In this way their children's generation becomes brighter, along with each successive generation. Ha! When I say "great being," you think of someone who wears the gray clothes of a Buddhist monk or nun, don't you? But these aren't required for someone to be a great being.

---

12. Karmic affinity(因緣): The connection or attraction between people or things, due to previous karmic relationships.

보살의 행은 남을 조금이라도 해롭게 해서도 아니 되지마는 이익 하게 하지 않는다면 그건 도가 아니요, 심부름꾼이 될 수 없습니다. 우주천지에서 인정을 해 주지 않습니다. 인정을 해 주지 않기 때문에 권리가 쥐어지지 않는 거죠. 보살의 행도 권리가 있어야만이 할 수 있는 거지 아무나 하는 게 아닙니다. 이렇게 진정한 심부름꾼이 된다면 조상들도 모두 문이 열리고 귀가 트이고 눈이 떠지고 지역지역 어디든지 한마음으로 통신이 되어, 각각의 연유로 인해 갇혀있는 영령들을 깨워 제 갈 길을 가게 할 수 있습니다.

Following the path of the *Bodhisattvas*[13] means not harming others in the slightest. But more than that, it means that what you do to others must only benefit them. Otherwise, it will be impossible for you to fulfill the role of a Bodhisattva. Why? Because the universe won't give you its approval, and so it also won't give you its authority, which is necessary to truly fulfill the role of a Bodhisattva. The actions of a Bodhisattva aren't something you can do just because you want to. When we can truly run errands on behalf of the whole, then we can open the door for all of our ancestors, and open their eyes and ears. We can communicate as one with everything in everyplace we visit, and so can free the spirits of the dead who are trapped in those places. We can wake them up from the thoughts they're trapped in, allowing them to go forward on their own path.

When I went to Germany and was staying at our center there, the spirit of a nun abruptly

---

13. Bodhisattva: In the most basic sense, a Bodhisattva is a manifestation of Buddha, which helps save beings and also uses the non-dual wisdom of enlightenment to help them awaken for themselves.

이번에 이런 일이 있었죠. 독일에 가서 지원에 묵고 있는데 난데없이 수녀 한 분이 들어왔어요. 들어와서 무슨 역사에 대해 뭐라고 하는데, 나는 무식해서 그냥 때에 따라 역사도 알게 되면 아는 거라, 그냥 듣다가 누구냐고 물으니까, 삼백사오십 년 이전에 있었던 사람이라고 하는 겁니다. 그래서 왜 나한테 왔느냐고 그랬어요. 그러자 이런 얘기를 하는 겁니다.

종교 싸움으로 인해서 많은 독일 사람들이 죽었는데 그때 자기들은 예배당 같은 것 하나 조그맣게 해 놓고 그 일판에 있던 세 개의 큰 천막에서 죽어가는 사람들을 치료해줬다 합니다. 그러다 막판에 가서는 뭇사람들한테 봉변을 당해 그 자리에 묻혔다고 했습니다. 그런데 그 수녀뿐만 아니라 그 일대에서 고문 당하다 죽은 사람들이 그 자리에 갇혀 한 발짝도 떼어 놓을 수가 없어 그대로 있다고 하는 겁니다. 그러니 나보고 이왕 여기 왔으니 자기네 문을 열어 줄 수 없냐고 묻더라구요.

appeared before me. She started talking at length about some historical event that I'd never heard of. There are actually lots of things I don't know about, but if I encounter them, and need to know about them, then they become clear to me. Anyway, I just listened for a while, and then asked who she was. She answered, "I lived here about three hundred and fifty years ago." So I changed direction and asked her why she'd come to visit me. She told me the following story:

"At the time I lived here, there was a huge religious war that killed nearly half the people in the land. So many people were sick, starving, or injured in those days that we nuns, who ran the chapel that used to be here, set up three large nursing camps. We raised awnings to shelter people from the sun and rain, and we cared for the sick and dying as best we could. However, in the end many people came and abused us horribly. They killed us, and we were buried on this spot. Many others were also tortured and killed here, and buried with us. From that time until now, we haven't been able to leave this place. Since you've come here, can you help us leave? Can you open the door for us?"

그래서 "아이구, 이게 무슨 소리야? 부처님 법에서나 가톨릭 법에서나 사람은 다르지 않아. 모두가 둘이 아니라서 당신도 할 수 있어. 뭐하러 나한테 부탁을 하나?"라고 죽 설명을 해줬습니다. 그랬더니 그 소리를 퍼뜩 알아 듣고선 부처님 모셔 놓은 데에 가서 삼배를 올리고 수녀의 옷을 벗어서 담 너머로 다 팽개쳤습니다.

그러면 영령들이 갇혀서 제 갈 길을 못 가는 경우가 애초에 왜 생기느냐 하는 것도 문제지만, 이러한 많은 영령들이 한꺼번에 천도되어야 하는 문제가 이렇게 오리라고 생각을 했기 때문에 국내외적으로 여러 군묘지를 택해서 해보고, 또 이곳 저곳에서 이름 없이 죽어간 영령들을 운집해서 길을 열어 주기도 한 것입니다. 오는 사람만 건지는 게 부처님의 가르침이 아닙니다.

"Oh my dear," I replied, "you've got it backwards. In both Catholic and Buddhist teachings, everyone is interconnected. No one is separate from anyone else, so why would you need me to open the door for you?" I then explained at length to her about this one mind that connects us all.

After hearing this, she ran to the Dharma Hall, bowed three times, and then threw her nun's robes over the garden wall. [Next to the Dharma Hall there is a large area of grass and garden that is enclosed by a concrete wall.]

While we need to understand why spirits get stuck like this and can't move forward, it's also important to be able to free them as a group. A long time ago, I saw that at military cemeteries there were many spirits stuck there, unable to move forward. I realized that I needed to be able to gather them all together and free them so that they could each go forward on their own path. To this end, I practiced doing this at cemeteries, and especially at military cemeteries both in Korea and overseas. We need to be able to save all beings, even those who don't realize they are stuck. It would not be in accord with the Buddha's

몸 하나를 건지면 그 속에 들어 있는 중생들을 다 살릴 수 있습니다. 그러니까 그렇게 영령들의 문을 열어 주고 구해 주는 것도 여러분이 그러한 마음공부[10]를 해야 가능한 것입니다. 영령들은 다 압니다, 누가 자기를 이익 하게 할 수 있는지. 그걸 알기 때문에 찾아오는 것입니다.

마음은 빛보다 더 빠릅니다. 마음은 체가 없고 광대무변하고 묘합니다. 여러분은 이렇게 귀중한 마음을 허투루 두지 말고 하나로 뭉쳐, 그 한마음에서 검부락지 하나를 일으켜 세운다 하더라도 그것로 지구를 들 수 있는 그런 태세라야만이 되겠습니다. 이런 이치가 있기에 이날까지 여러분한테 간곡히 마음공부를 하시도록 가르쳐 왔던 겁니다.

지금 지구의 오염이 점점 심각해지고 있습니다. 나는 무식해서 학계에서 쓰는 언어는 잘 모릅니다. 지구의 오염이 심해져서 지구를 둘러싸고 있는 공기가 너무 더워지면 공기막이 터져 지구에 큰 재앙이 올 수 있습니다.

---

10. 마음공부: 진정한 자유인이 되기 위해 자신의 마음이 어떻게 작용하고 변하는지를 관찰하고 배우며, 그것을 실제 생활 속에서 응용하고 체험해 보면서 알아가는 모든 과정을 뜻함.

teachings to think of only those beings who come to you looking for help.

If you save one body, you instantly save all of the beings within it. It's like this. Your ability to set all those spirits free depends upon your ability to rely upon your own fundamental mind, and through that, to become one with everything. Spirits appear because they know who can help them. Those spirits aren't walking to you, or taking steps one at a time. They appear instantly, because mind moves instantly.

Please don't treat this fundamental mind of ours as if it was something you could ignore, or something that's not particularly relevant to you. No matter what, you must practice gathering everything together in your fundamental mind, until even a small, quiet thought entrusted there can come back out and move the entire world. This is why I keep teaching and imploring you to learn to rely upon your fundamental mind.

Currently, all over the world, pollution is becoming worse than ever before. I don't know the proper scientific terms for these things, but if the pollution worsens, the atmosphere will heat up and holes will form in the layers that protect

물난리도 날 수 있구요. 또 지금 오염 그 자체도 큰 문제죠. 지구가 이렇게 오염이 되면 가차없이 모두가 살림을 다시 해야 합니다. 그런데 뭔가를 버려서만이 오염이 되는 게 아니라, 예를 들어 알프스 산에 케이블카를 설치하느라 땅을 파고 쇳덩어리를 박고 이런 것도 벌써 오염이에요. 자연을 파괴시키는 게 오염이란 말입니다.

완전히 잘 배운 의사는 수술을 할 때에 잘라야 할 곳만 자릅니다. 그런데 그런 것도 모르고 세포고 동맥이고 뭐고 할 거 없이 막 끊고 쇠를 박으니 이게 오염이 아니고 뭐겠습니까? 의사도 아니면서 의사 노릇을 하는 그런 사람들로 인해서 생기는 오염의 심각성을 아십니까? 그 오염을 막는 것도 우리 마음에 달려 있습니다. 끊어진 세포를 잇는 것도 우리의 마음에 달려 있고요. 하여튼 마음은 광대무변합니다. 이건 뭐든지 할 수 있다는 겁니다. 그 오염을 전체 깨끗하게 막아준다면 문제는 달라집니다.

the atmosphere. This would open the way for enormous calamities to happen, including major flooding. Even now pollution is causing serious problems. If it continues, we'll have to completely start our lives over again from nothing. Garbage and such isn't the only source of pollution. For example, in the Alps they've planted great steel pillars for cable cars, and these, too, are a form of pollution.

Skilled doctors will cut away only the damaged parts. But would you want to go under the knife of a doctor who never went to medical school and doesn't even know anatomy? Now we have people who can't tell the difference between a vein and an artery cutting into mountains and planting steel pillars every which way. How could this not be pollution? Can you imagine the damage being done by people who think they're doctors, but who can't even tell left from right?

However, even that damage, that pollution, can be prevented if we use our minds wisely. It is also our minds that can reconnect those cells that have been cut off. The ability of this fundamental mind of ours is so vast and incredible; it can truly do anything.

우리 몸 안에 창자나 대장 같은 여러 내장기관이 있어 서로 소통되듯이 지구도 마찬가지입니다. 남극과 북극이 통하는 통로도 있고 분비물이 나가게 할 수 있는 통로도 있습니다. 지금의 상식으로는 곳곳이 비었다 차있다 어떻게 말을 해야 할지 모르겠지만, 달도 그렇고 해도 그렇고 그러한 공간이 있어서 양쪽으로 들이고 내는 그 소통이 아주 정연하게 돼 있기 때문에, 너무 팽창되지도 않고 너무 타 버리지도 않게끔 되는 것입니다. 이렇게 소통이 잘돼서 수명이 길게 되고, 잘 안돼서 짧게 되는 것도 우리 마음에 달려 있다 이겁니다. 지구의 수명을 단축시키고 결과적으로 우리의 지구를 파괴시키는 이 오염을 전체 깨끗하게 막아준다면 문제는 달라집니다. 그것은 전체 우리 마음이 은하계와 결부돼 있기 때문입니다. 내가 여러분한테 옛날에 이런 애길 잘 하지 않는 이유는 '저 미친 중이야!' 이러면서 받아들이는 걸 힘들어하기 때문입니다. 내가 옛날에도 "지구도 달도 비었다. 모든 게 꽉 차 있다고 생각을 한다면 큰 오산이다."라고 말했었습니다.

Within our bodies, the intestines, colon, and other organs communicate and work with each other to enable us to live. The Earth is also like this, and has a channel connecting the North Pole with the South Pole, and a channel that works to process and excrete waste products.

The words "hollow" and "solid" as they are normally understood don't quite fit here. I'm not sure of the right words or scientific concepts I need to properly express this, but the moon and the sun also have such "channels," which allow them to function properly. These also keep the sun from expanding too much or burning too quickly. When these channels function smoothly, the life of planets and suns is long, but when they don't, their life becomes shortened. How well these function depends upon how we use our minds. It is like this because our minds and the universe are linked together. How well we use our minds is also what determines whether pollution harms us or not.

I rarely spoke of these things in the past because people have a hard time accepting them. Instead, they tended to just call me crazy and ignore what I was saying. This also

화성에도 사람이 살았었는데 살 수 없는 환경이 되면서 숨 쉴 수 있는 공기가 없어지게 되었습니다. 이건 화성이 오염되면서 문제가 일어났던 겁니다. 지금은 생명체가 좀 살아나고 있죠. 그것은 우리들의 마음에 생명이 자라게 하려면 자라게 하고, 또, 생명이 없어지게 하려면 없어지게 하고, 물이 생기게 하려면 생기게 하는, 그런 자유가 있기 때문입니다. 자유권을 여러분이 가졌습니다. 자기를 무시하지 마세요. 자기를 무시하는 것은 자기를 있게 한 불성, 그 부처를 무시하는 거와 똑같습니다. 우리가 어떻게 해서 이렇게 살고 있는지도 모르면서 그냥 죽을 수는 없죠. 죽는 게 아까워서가 아닙니다. 마음공부를 하지 않으면 우리가 바닥부터 새로 살림을 해야 하는 너무나 처참한 문제가 있고, 또 하나는 내 부모, 네 부모가 따로 없다는 사실을 모르고 죽으면 개인적으로도 득 될 게 하나도 없습니다. 우리가 미생물에서부터 항상 둘이 아니라고 했죠?

happened when I said that the Earth and moon are both "hollow," and that it was a significant misunderstanding to think of them as being utterly filled with solids or liquids.

Beings once lived on Mars as well, but the air disappeared and made it impossible to live there. This happened as the pollution became severe. But lives are gradually appearing now, because our minds have the ability to cause life to appear or to disappear. Likewise, if we want water to be there, it gradually appears. You all have the freedom to do this. Don't disregard yourself. If you look down upon yourself, it's the same as looking down upon the fundamental Buddha-nature that's been guiding you. We can't just continue to live and die in *ignorance*[14] of our fundamental nature. Dying isn't the problem. The real problem is that, first, if everyone continues on like this, eventually the whole world will have to start over from the cold, harsh beginning. Second, if you die without knowing that everything is

---

14. Ignorance(無明)**:** Literally this means darkness. It is the unenlightened mind that does not see the truth. It is being unaware of the inherent oneness of all things, and it is the fundamental cause of birth, aging, sickness, and death.

미생물에서부터 부모가 되고 자식이 되고 형제가 되고 하면서 형성돼 올라왔고 진화돼 올라왔기 때문에 그렇다고요.

그러니까 이 마음공부를 할 수 있는 사람이라면 여러분의 이름은 벌써 우주에 다 기록이 돼 있다는 걸 아셔야 합니다. 거짓말 같죠? 거짓말이 아니에요. 보이는 데 글자 쓰는 것만 글자가 아닙니다.

하여튼 이러한 이유가 있기에 마음공부를 꼭 해야 한다는 겁니다. 전에 우리 스님들이 폼페이인가 어디 외국에 간 적이 있었는데 물로 죽고 불로 죽고 하던 시대에 있었던 영가들이 나와서 천도해 주기를 바라더랍니다. 그래서 상 차리고 재 올리느라 한잠도 못 자고 아침까지 하고 왔다고 그러더라구요. 그 말을 듣고 내가 그랬죠. "그렇게 밤까지 샐 게 뭐 있니? 이 종지의 물도(법상 위의 컵을 가리키며) 바다에 넣으면 바닷물이 되는 건데. 그냥 마음에 다 담으면 되는 거지. 마음은 한계가 없다. 제사상에도 이 세상 거를 다 갖나 놓을 수 있지 않겠느냐?"

one, that everyone's parents are your own parents, you won't see any improvement in your next life. From the very beginning, throughout our entire evolution, we've always been connected to every other life. My parents aren't separate from your parents – everyone has been our parents, our children, our brothers, and our sisters.

If you are someone who is able to rely upon your fundamental mind, then your name is already known throughout the universe and the upper realms. Some of your faces say that you think I'm making all of this up, but I'm not. It is really true. Not everything that is written down and recorded is visible to your eyes.

Again, I can't emphasize enough how important it is to learn to rely upon our fundamental mind. When some of our sunims were visiting Pompeii, they were asked for help by the spirits of those who died by fire and drowning a very long time ago. So the sunims stayed up all night trying to help them. When they came back and told me this, I said, "Why was staying up all night necessary? Look at the water in this cup; if it's added to the sea, it becomes the sea. All those spirits can become your mind in an instant,

이미 죽은 영가들은 이렇게 해서 어느 정도 구제받을 수 있겠지만 우리는 우리가 왜 이렇게 마음공부를 해야만 하는지 알고는 가야죠. 여러분이 이렇게 마음공부를 하면 내가 사는 이 집을 길이길이 보존할 수 있고, 동시에 그 차원이 정말이지 우수해져서 세세생생을 얻을 수가 있다는 그 사실도 또 덧붙여 아셔야 됩니다.

　　어느 스님이 이렇게 묻더군요. "스님은 왜 우주떡 하나를 해 놓고 천도를 하십니까?" 이러길래 "이번 한 생뿐만 아니라 수억 겁을 내려오면서 먹고, 벌고, 파고, 입고, 싸우고, 죽고 이러면서 살아오지 않았습니까? 그러니 영가들의 그 의식을 면제해 주려면 아주 우주에다 집어넣어서 '너 마음대로 먹고 너 마음대로 해라.'고 한다면 복잡할 게 없지 않습니까? 공(空)한 줄 알게 되면 아무것도 아닙니다. 우리가 막말로 에너지만 돌려쓸 줄 알면 그뿐인데 뭘 그렇게 어렵고 복잡하게 그럽니까?"라고 말을 했죠.

so what's left to do? Mind has no limitation. Offerings of fruit or flowers – anything at all – can be done through mind.

Practicing like this, you can help free the spirits of the dead, but there's something that's even more important: While practicing with the things that come up in your life, and learning to entrust them to your fundamental mind, you can also protect this place we live in and ensure that it flourishes for a long time. Practicing like this, you'll continue to raise your spiritual level, and reach the point where the brightness you've attained will never, ever fade.

A sunim asked why, unlike other temples, we don't have huge tables of food when we have a ceremony to help the dead. I answered that for eons we've struggled to eat, to obtain, and to dig, all the while fighting and dying, and constantly getting a new body. So in order to help dissolve these states of consciousness, you should just put those spirits into the energy of the universe and tell them to eat as much as they want, and to do whatever they would like to. If you can do this, helping the dead is very straightforward. It's not complicated if you truly understand that

법당에 부처님 모셔 놓은 것은 보기 좋으라고 그냥 해 놓는 게 아닙니다. 부처님 한 분 모셔 놓으려면 얼마나 눈물겨운 뼈저린 아픔이 있어야 하는데 그렇게 모셔 놓겠습니까? 부처님 한 몸이 여러분의 몸도 될 수 있고 내 몸도 될 수 있음을 알게 하기 위해서입니다.

우리가 이 공부할 때 정신계로 들어가라고 하니까 어떤 사람들은 공(空)에 빠져서 물질계는 우습게 생각하는데, 여러분 자체만 보더라도 물질계와 정신계가 둘이 아니라는 것을 알 겁니다, 아마. 여러분의 정신이 빠져도 육신은 송장이 되니 무효고, 또 정신계만 있으면 보이지 않아서 무효고. 그러면 어떻게 해야 옳을까요? 정상체(定常體)로 있으려면 정신계와 물질계가 혼합이 돼서 둘 아니게 사셔야 되는 거 아닙니까? 그런데 부처와 중생이 따로 있는 걸로 알고, 정신계와 물질계가 따로 있는 걸로 알고, 부처의 몸과 우리의 몸이 따로 있는 걸로 아시는데 그거는 아닙니다.

everything is constantly changing and flowing as one whole. To put it bluntly, if you can freely use the infinite energy that always surrounds us, there's no need for table after table of offerings.

Our sunims go through so many hardships when they build a new Dharma hall, don't they? So much sincerity and good intention goes into the construction process and finding just the right Buddha statue. All of this is to help teach people that the mind of Buddha can become one with you and I.

As we practice, we're trying to take care of the things in our lives while being grounded in the spiritual realm. However, sometimes this causes people to make the mistake of looking down upon the material realm. As you reflect upon yourself, all of you probably understand that the material and spiritual realms work together as one. Without consciousness, your body would be just a corpse. And if you didn't have a body, what could your consciousness do? How could you lead a normal existence unless the spiritual realm and the material realm were functioning as one combined whole?

'부처님의 몸도 자기 몸과 같이 생각하라. 부처님의 마음도 자기 마음같이 생각하라. 또 부처님의 법도 자기 생활의 법과 같이 생각하라. 아래로는 내 아픔이 전체의 아픔인 줄 알고 살아라. 모두가 내 몸 아님이 없고 내 부모 아님이 없고 내 자식 아님이 없으니 분별하지 말라.'고 석가모니 부처님도 이렇게 말씀해 놓으셨죠.

그런데 내가 무식한 게 여러분한테 다행이에요. 왠 줄 아십니까? 내가 유식했으면 말입니다, 이렇게 말 안 하거든요? 직선적으로 그냥 무식한 대로 이렇게 내질러서 말을 하지 않고 아주 지식적이고 학술적으로 잘 만들어서 착 내놓죠. 하하하…… 그런데 나는 워낙 촌에서 호미자루만 들고 밭 매던 사람과 같기 때문에 무댓방 내가 아는 대로 그냥 그냥 얘기하는 거예요. 그러니까 여러분한테 상당히 쉽단 말입니다, 알아듣기가. 안 그렇습니까? 그러니까 내가 무식한 게 되레 여러분한테 이익이죠. 허허허……

지금 이 우주에 관한 건도 말 못할 문제가 너무도 많습니다. 혹자는 우리가 이런 거에 관해 말을 하면 그 말뿐이 아니라 그로 인해 먹은 마음 때문에 마(魔)가 들까 염려를 하기도 하지만, 이것은 귀신이든 사람이든 어떤 영가든 둘 아니게

Nonetheless, people think that Buddhas exist apart from themselves, that the spiritual realm exists apart from the material realm, and that the Buddha's body exists apart from our body. But all of this is wrong. Know that the body of Buddha is your own body. Know that the mind of Buddha is your own mind. Know that the truth the Buddha taught exists throughout every part and instant of your daily life. Further, know that if you are in pain, the whole knows of your pain. Everyone is your parent; everyone is your own child. So, don't get caught up in the trap of discriminations. This is also what Shakyamuni Buddha taught.

You know, as I think about it, my lack of education has worked out really well for all of you! If I'd had an education, I might be trying to explain this in terms of theory, with all kinds of long, scholarly words. Instead, because I never went to school, I can speak to you directly, in terms we can all understand. I'm like a village farmer who doesn't know how to beat around the bush! [Laughs.]

There are many, many things happening with our world and universe, and most of them I can't reveal to you because people aren't ready to hear

다루는 멋있는 법이라서 그런 염려는 안 해도 됩니다. 단지 여러분이 그것을 듣고 소화를 못 시키고 '정말 저이가 성한 사람인가?' 이런 생각만 할까 봐 더는 그 말을 못 합니다. 또 나중에는 모르죠, 여러분이 그거를 집어 넣고도 다 소화를 시킬 수 있다면 그땐 말해도 될지 모르죠. 그런데 현재 우리 상황이 급박하니까, 지금 다 말할 수 없는 그 문제들을 여러분이 이해할 수 없다는 이유로 외면해서는 안되고, 그것이 다 소화가 될 정도로 우리가 마음공부를 열심히 하지 않으면 안됩니다.

그뿐만 아니라 우리 개인에 관해서도 생각해 봅시다. 천차만별 차원의 종자가 있는데 그중의 한 종자가 차원이 높아져 그 껍질이 아주 그냥 깎이고 깎이고 깎여, 지금은 붙지 않는 하늘이지만, 그 하늘에 닿게 할 수 있는 큰 배나무가 됐다고 합시다. 그 배나무에 잘 여문 누런 배 다섯 개가 이렇게 열려 있는데 그것 한번 생각해 보세요. 그 나무가 다른 생명을 뜯어 먹고 그렇게 훌륭하게 자란 겁니까? 꼿꼿하게 올라가서 우주를 삼킬 수 있는 큰 배들이 열렸는데 그것이 자기라고 생각했을 때 어떻습니까?

about them. Perhaps later, when you can digest this, I can say more about them. Even among the things I've mentioned, some people worry that if we talk about those, or think too much about them, then our words and thoughts will cause those harmful things to come true. However there's no need to worry about such things when you understand this beautiful, non-dual practice, for it can handle all problems, even those of the living and the dead.

When I talk about these things, I can feel that many people can't take in what I'm saying. So I usually don't want to talk too much about them because I'm concerned that people will think I'm crazy, and so won't try to practice. The current situation is quite urgent; everyone needs to work on their practice until they are able to understand and respond to these issues. Don't turn away from these problems, excusing yourself with a "well, it's beyond my understanding...."

Look at what happens on an individual level: among all the many different kinds of seeds, one begins to raise its level and peels off its shell time after time. Even though it was stuck in the dirt, it became a great pear tree that eventually reached

나는 항상 그 나무들은 이 세상을 주고도 바꿀 수가 없다고 그럽니다. 여러분이 그런 나무로 화(化)해서 등장을 하신다면 한 손가락뿐만 아니라 한 검부락지만으로도 이 우주를 아마 잘 보존해서 들 수 있을 겁니다. 어때요? 여러분이 그렇게 일을 한다면 무(無)의 수행자일 뿐만 아니라 무의 과학자도 되는 겁니다. 하지만 물질만을 보고 따지는 유(有)의 과학자는 그렇게 될 수가 없죠. 일이 벌어지는 걸 볼 수는 있지만 보고도 그냥 어쩔 수가 없게 되는 거죠.

물컵이 쓰러져 물이 쏟아질 걸 알면 그렇게 될 거라고 얘기만 하는 게 아니라 그렇게 되지 않도록 할 수 있어야 합니다. 그러니까 될 수 있으면 우리는 그렇게 할 수 있다는 것을 명심하세요. 그뿐만 아니라 소소한 일이라도 보이지 않는 데서부터 보이는 데로 나오는 것이고, 또 보이는 데서 우리가 눈으로 보고 귀로 듣고 이렇게 행하는 것이 모두 무(無)에 또 입력이 된다는 것도 명심하시고요.

the heavens, and has five great, golden pears hanging from it. Did that pear tree grow into such a magnificent tree by tearing apart and eating other living beings? No. It grows uprightly, and those huge pears can swallow even the universe. Now what would you think if I told you that the tree and those pears were you yourself?

There's nothing in the universe that can replace trees like these. If you can become such a tree, you can move the entire world using nothing more than the tiniest of things. At this point, you will be a practitioner who functions throughout the unseen realm, and a scientist who brings forth what is needed into the visible realm. This is vastly beyond the abilities of those scientists who do everything based upon only the material realm. Even when they can see something starting to happen, they can't do anything about it.

If you could foresee that a cup of water is about to fall and break, is that enough? What you should do is prevent it from happening. Although this may seem hard to believe, please keep in mind that all of you have the ability to do this. Even small and trivial things begin at the unseen realm and then manifest into the visible world.

비가 오나 눈이 오나 잠이 드나 일을 하나, 모든 것을 보이지 않는 그 자리에서 한다고 생각하라고 이렇게 말을 하는 것은 바로 그 까닭입니다. 여러분이 이 세상을 좋게 살릴 수 있고, 이 세상의 모든 생명들을 건질 수 있습니다. 하나하나 오는 사람만 건지는 게 아니라, 모두를 다 건질 수 있습니다. 진화시키고 창조해서, 그것도 누가 했다 누가 했다 이런 말 없이 그냥 묵묵히 그렇게 할 수 있는 사람이라면 이 세상에서만이 아니라 아예 우주에서 상을 받아요, 그냥. 여러분 질문하실 게 없어요?

사회자: 오늘 질문이 없는 것 같습니다.

큰스님: 사람이 이렇게 많이 있는데 질문이 왜 없습니까? 잘하든 못하든 (내면에서) 올라오는 궁금증이 진짜 질문이지 일부러 만들어 가지고 하는 거는 진짜가 아닙니다. 질문이 진짜가 아니라면 대답도 아마 진짜가 아닐는지도 모르죠. 하하하……

Likewise, our reactions to everything we see, hear, and feel are all input into the unseen realm.

This is why I keep saying that we have to remind ourselves that no matter the circumstances we find ourselves in – pleasant or difficult, whether we are awake or asleep – they are all being done by our fundamental mind. You all are the ones who can make this world into a wonderful place to live, and you are the ones who can save all the life on this world. And I don't mean just those beings who come to you looking for help. You are the one who can save all beings, even those who don't know they're stuck. If you can quietly work through the unseen realm to help them evolve, and can do this without talking or boasting about it, you will definitely receive an award from the Earth, as well as the universe!

Are there no questions today? No one has anything to ask? Whether your question seems stupid or not, if it's a question that wells up from within you, then that's true question. If you overthink it and try to come up with a "good" question, that will actually be a fake question. And if you ask me a fake question, you may get a fake answer! [Laughs.]

살면서, 아픈 때도 많고, 슬플 때도 많고, 허망할 때도 많고, 짜증날 때도 많고, 화가 날 때도 많고, 살기 싫은 때도 많을 겁니다. 하지만 우리는 이렇게 살아 있습니다. 누가 살아라 말아라 하지 않아도 생생히 살아 있기 때문에 사는 겁니다. 그러니 어떡합니까, 잘 살아야죠. 하하하…… (대중 웃음 후 합장하시며) 한 분도 질문할 게 없어요? 당신은 왜 그렇게 미친 소리만 하느냐고 질문 안 해요? (대중 웃음) 하하하…… 그런데 미친 짓은 나 혼자만 하는 게 아니라 전체, 일체가 다 지금 미친 짓을 하고 가고 있어요. 급하니까요, 모두가. 점차적으로 다가오거든요, 급하게요. 그러니까 우리는 하늘이 무너져도 싱긋이 웃을 수 있을 정도가 되야 된다는 말입니다. (대중 박수) 질문이 없다니 제가 해외지원에 법회하러 갔을 때 얘기를 해드릴게요.

　얼마 전에 캐나다에 갔었는데 신문사에서 사진 찍는 사람이 와서 나를 계속 쫓아다니는 거예요. 저수지엘 가도 쫓아오고, 산엘 가도 쫓아오고, 어딜 가도 쫓아오는데, 하여튼 그 사람이 그렇게 착할 수가 없어요. 한편으론 조신하기도 하고요. 자상하다고나 할까요? 쫓아다니는 게 말입니다. 하하하…… 내가 한국에 먼저 왔습니다. 그 사람은 아마 오늘 올 거예요.

We all go through difficult times of illness, loneliness, hopelessness, stress, frustration, and even times when you wish you could die. But we are nonetheless alive here now. So, we may as well live wisely. What do you all think! [She puts her palms together in front of her.] So, no one wants to ask me why I talk about such strange things? [Laughs.] Sometimes people call me crazy, but it's the whole world that's doing crazy things. People's behavior is steadily worsening as the situation around the world becomes more desperate. This is why we need to deepen our practice to the point where we can just smile even if the heavens come crashing down.

If there are no questions, do you want to hear about the overseas branches? Okay. [She looks around.] When I was in Canada, there was a newspaper photographer who followed me everywhere, even when I went on a trip to the mountains. But he seemed very kind and gentle, and was always considerate about taking photos. I don't see him today, but then again, I wouldn't be surprised to hear that he's at the airport now!

참, 그 얘길 안 해 드렸네요. 독일에서도 법회를 했는데 대략 이백 명이 왔었어요. 대사나 공사, 이런 분들도 왔습니다. 거기는 불교라는 이름도 잘 모르고 뭐 하는 건지도 모르니까 스님네들이 밖으로 나가면 구경들을 해요. 그래서 내가 독일 말 하는 스님더러 그랬어요. "저 사람네들 구경하고도 구경 값을 안 내고 가니 무슨 연고냐고 물어라." 그 말을 독일 사람한테 전하니까, 그냥 아주 우스워 죽겠다고 그러더래요. 법회를 할 때는 독일 사람이 반 이상 와서 동시통역을 하면서 했습니다. 그렇게 해서 모두 잘 치뤘습니다. 독일지원도 아주 좋아요. 들어가면 정원이 집안 가운데 있는데, 지붕이 없어서 하늘하고 통하고, 또 집안에 연못이 있고 나무들이 있는데 사방을 유리로 막아서 바람이 불면 집안에서 나무가 흔들리는 것이 보여서 좋아요. 하여튼 절이 터도 널찍해서 좋아요.

캐나다는 한인회관을 사서 개조했는데 무척 넓어요. 법당도 넓고요. 불상을 모셔 놨는데 그렇게 정징하고 좋을 수가 없어요. 그리고 주차장이 아마 빌딩 하나는 세울 정도로 넓을 거에요. 그래서 좋구요. 거기다 천막을 쳤는데 한 천사백 명 정도 왔어요.

Ah, I forgot to tell you about the German Dharma talk. It went very well, with over two hundred people attending, including the Korean Ambassador. In Germany, people aren't used to seeing Buddhist nuns or monks, so wherever we went they would stop and stare at us. So, I smiled at one group and told them that if they were going to stare at us, then they should pay us something for having entertained them. Hearing the translation, those serious-looking people laughed so hard they almost cried!

At the talk we used a new system of simultaneous translation, which worked very well. The German center also looks very nice. There's small, square garden in the center of the house that's open to the sky and is almost a small courtyard. It's surrounded by glass walls, so you can sit in the house and look out at it. It was nice to watch the trees blow in the wind. The center is very pretty and has a large yard and garden next to the Dharma hall.

In Canada, we bought the building that used to be the center for the Korean Immigrants Association, and the space is huge! The newly installed Buddha statue was so pure and bright!

그리고 여러 나라 사람들도 왔는데 특히 이 마음공부 하는 사람들이 많이 왔어요. 어느 종교를 믿는 사람인지는 모르겠지만 머리를 칭칭 동여맨 외국 사람이 이 세상을 창조한 사람이 누구냐고 묻더라구요. 그래서 "네 놈이 했다." 그랬죠. (대중 웃음) 불이라는 놈하고, 물이라는 놈하고, 흙이란 놈하고, 바람이란 놈하고 그렇게 넷이서 창조를 했다구요.

내가 무식하길래 그 사람도 알아들었지 만약에 내가 유식했더라면 그 사람은 못 알아들었을 거에요. (대중 웃음) 하하하…… 아, 정말이에요. 부처님 법을 잘 아는 분들이 유식하게 외국말로 이 말을 하게 되면 그 사람이 알아들을 수가 없죠. 그런데 내가 단순 무식하게 그냥 물이다…… 이러고 얘길 하니까 아주 잘 알아듣고 얼마나 좋아하는지. 손을 번쩍 들고 좋아서 그냥 그러더군요. (대중 웃음)

어떨 때 보면 도둑질을 해도 크게 못 하고 조그맣게 하고 그러는데, 도둑질이 아닌 도둑질을 하려면 여러분도 나를 따라서 다 무식한 도둑놈이 돼 가지고, 이 세상을 홈빡 한 손가락 안에다

The building also came with a huge parking lot. So, for the opening they covered it with awnings and about 1,400 people came to hear the Dharma talk.

People from many different countries attended, and there were a lot of people who had some sense of living through our fundamental mind. One fellow wearing a turban asked me who created the universe. I said it was four guys named Fire, Water, Earth, and Air, who got together and created the world. [Laughs.]

He could understand my answer because I don't have any education. If I'd gone to school and was able to explain all of the deep meanings of this using the proper scientific and technical terms, people would have no idea what I'm talking about. [Laughs.] If I'd used the technical terms, people probably would have misunderstood me. Instead, I answered him very simply and directly, and when he heard my full answer, he clapped and raised his hands in the air.

If you want to attain something, then do it in a big way, so that you can truly make a difference in the world. Take everything in the entire world and utterly put it into this one place [holding up

넣으셔야 돼요. 그리고 소소한 거는 다 버리세요. 다 버려서 보이지 않는 그 자리에 놓으면 여러분의 것이 되는 거지 딴 데 가는 게 아니거든요, 그게. 버려도 그 자리에 있는 거지. 허허허…… 내가 지금 외국에 갔던 얘기 다 해 버리면 이다음에 재미가 없을 것 같아서 이걸로 끝내겠습니다.

one finger]. And take all those trivial things and throw them away. Don't worry about the things you let go of to this unseen place; they're still yours. [Laughs.]

Let's stop here for today; if I go on about my trip, we won't have anything fun to talk about next time!

한마음출판사의 마음을 밝혀주는 도서

- A Thousand Hands of Compassion
  만가지 꽃이 피고 만가지 열매 익어
  : 대행큰스님의 뜻으로 푼 천수경 (한글/영어)
   [2010 iF Communication Design Award 수상]

- Wake Up And Laugh (영어)

- No River To Cross, No Raft To Find (영어)

- It's Hard To Say (영어) (절판)

- My Heart Is A Golden Buddha (영어)

- Touching The Earth (영어) (2014 new)

- Moonlight In A Thousand Rivers (한글/영어) (2014 new)

- 생활 속의 참선수행 (시리즈) (한글/영어)
  1. 죽어야 나를 보리라
     (To Discover Your True Self, "I" Must Die)
  2. 함이 없이 하는 도리
     (Walking Without A Trace)
  3. 맡겨놓고 지켜봐라
     (Let Go And Observe)
  4. 마음은 보이지 않는 행복의 창고
     (Mind, Treasure House Of Happiness)
  5. 일체를 용광로에 넣어라
     (The Furnace Within Yourself)
  6. 온 우주를 살리는 마음의 불씨
     (The Spark That Can Save The Universe, 2014 new edition)
  7. 한마음의 위력
     (The Infinite Power Of One Mind, 2014 new)
  8. 일체를 움직이는 그 자리
     (In The Heart Of A Moment, 2014 new)

9. 한마음 한뜻이 되어
     (One With The Universe, 2014 new)
  10. 지구 보존
     (Protecting The Earth, 2014 new)

- 내 마음은 금부처 (한글)

- 건널 강이 어디 있으랴 (한글)

  El Camino Interior (스페인어)

- Vida De La Maestra Seon Daehaeng (스페인어)

- Enseñanzas De La Maestra Daehaeng (스페인어)

- Práctica Del Seon En La Vida Diaria (Colección) (스페인어/영어)
  1. Una Semilla Inherente Alimenta El Universo
     (The Spark That Can Save The Universe)

- Si Te Lo Propones, No Hay Imposibles (스페인어)

- 人生不是苦海 (번체자 중국어) (2014 new edition)

- 无河可渡 (간체자 중국어) (2014 new)

- 我心是金佛 (간체자 중국어) (2014 new)

외국출판사에서 출판된 한마음도서

- Wake Up And Laugh
  Wisdom Publications, 미국

- No River To Cross
  (*No River To Cross, No Raft To Find* 영어판)
  Wisdom Publications, 미국

- Wie Flieβendes Wasser
  (*My Heart Is A Golden Buddha* 독일어판)
  Goldmann Arkana-Random House, 독일

- Ningún Río Que Cruzar
  (*No River To Cross* 스페인어판)
  Kailas Editorial, S.L., 스페인

- Umarmt Von Mitgefühl
  ('만가지 꽃이 피고 만가지 열매 익어':
  대행큰스님의 뜻으로 푼 천수경 독일어판)
  Diederichs-Random House, 독일

- 我心是金佛
  (*My Heart Is A Golden Buddha* 번체자 중국어판)
  橡樹林文化出版, 대만

- Vertraue Und Lass Alles Los
  (*No River To Cross* 독일어판)
  Goldmann Arkana-Random House, 독일

- Wache Auf Und Lache
  (*Wake Up And Laugh* 독일어판)
  Theseus, 독일

- Дзэн И Просветление
  (No River To Cross 러시아어판)
  Amrita-Rus, 러시아

- Sup Cacing Tanah
  (*My Heart Is A Golden Buddha* 인도네시아어판)
  PT Gramedia, 인도네시아

- Không có sông nào để vượt qua
  (*No River To Cross* 베트남어판)
  Phuong Nam Books, 베트남 (2014 출판예정)

- *No River To Cross*
  (*No River To Cross* 아랍어판, 제목미상)
  Sphinx Publishing, 이집트 (2015 출판예정)

Books by Daehaeng Kun Sunim
-available through Hanmaum Publications

- A Thousand Hands of Compassion (bilingual, Korean/English)
  [received **2010 iF communication design Award**]
- Wake Up And Laugh (English)
- No River To Cross, No Raft To Find (English)
- My Heart Is A Golden Buddha (English)
- Touching The Earth (English) (Forthcoming 2014)
- Moonlight In A Thousand Rivers
  (bilingual, Korean/English) (Forthcoming 2014)
- *Practice in Daily Life* (Series) (bilingual, Korean/English)
  1. To Discover Your True Self, "I" Must Die
  2. Walking Without A Trace
  3. Let Go And Observe
  4. Mind, Treasure House Of Happiness
  5. The Furnace Within Yourself
  6. The Spark That Can Save The Universe
  7. The Infinite Power Of One Mind
  8. In The Heart Of A Moment
  9. One With The Universe (Forthcoming 2014)
  10. Protecting The Earth (Forthcoming 2014)
- 건널 강이 어디 있으랴 (Korean)
- 내 마음은 금부처 (Korean)
- El Camino Interior (Spanish)
- Vida De La Maestra Seon Daehaeng (Spanish)
- Enseñanzas De La Maestra Daehaeng (Spanish)

- Práctica Del Seon En La Vida Diaria (Series) (bilingual, Spanish/English)
    1. Una Semilla Inherente Alimenta El Universo
- Si Te Lo Propones, No Hay Imposibles (Spanish)
- 人牛不是苦海 (Traditional Chinese)
- 无河可渡 (Simplified Chinese)
- 我心是金佛 (Simplified Chinese) (Forthcoming 2014)

-Books available through other Publishers

- No River To Cross
  Wisdom Publications, U.S.A.

- Wake Up And Laugh
  Wisdom Publications, U.S.A.

- Wie Flieβendes Wasser
  German edition of *My Heart Is A Golden Buddha*
  Goldmann Arkana-Random House, Germany

- Vertraue Und Lass Alles Los
  German edition of *No River To Cross*
  Goldmann Arkana-Random House, Germany

- Umarmt Von Mitgefühl
  German edition of *A Thousand Hands Of Compassion*
  Diederichs-Random House, Germany

- Wache Auf Und Lache
  German edition of *Wake Up And Laugh*
  Theseus, Germany

- Ningún Río Que Cruzar
  Spanish edition of *No River To Cross*
  Kailas Editorial, S.L., Spain

- 我心是金佛
  Traditional Chinese edition of *My Heart Is A Golden Buddha*
  Oak Tree Publishing Co., Taiwan

- Дзэн И Просветление
  Russian edition of *No River To Cross*
  Amrita-Rus, Russia

- Sup Cacing Tanah
  Indonesian edition of *My Heart Is A Golden Buddha*
  PT Gramedia, Indonesia

- Không có sông nào để vượt qua
  Vietnam edition of *No River To Cross*
  Phuong Nam Books, Vietnam, Forthcoming 2014

- *No River To Cross* (*title to be determined*)
  Arabic edition of *No River To Cross*
  Sphinx Publishing, Egypt, Forthcoming 2015

한마음선원본원

경기도 안양시 만안구 석수동 101-62
Tel : 82-31-470-3100   Fax : 82-31-470-3116
홈페이지 : http://www.hanmaum.org
이메일 : jongmuso@hanmaum.org

국내지원

강릉지원 (우)210-940 강원도 강릉시 포남2동 1304
TEL:(033) 651-3003   FAX:(033) 652-0281

공주지원 (우)314-870 충청남도 공주시 사곡면 신영3리 152-3
TEL:(041) 852-9100   FAX:(041) 852-9105

광명선원 (우)369-900 충청북도 음성군 금왕읍 대금로 1402번지
TEL:(043) 877-5000   FAX:(043) 877-2900

광주지원 (우)502-270 광주광역시 서구 치평동 201-5
TEL:(062) 373-8801   FAX:(062) 373-0174

대구지원 (우)706-838 대구광역시 수성구 수성로 41길 76번지
TEL:(053) 767-3100   FAX:(053) 765-1600

목포지원 (우)530-490 전라남도 목포시 상동 952-19
TEL:(061) 284-1771   FAX:(061) 284-1770

문경지원 (우)745-823 경상북도 문경시 신앙면 반곡리 449번지
TEL:(054) 555-8871   FAX:(054) 556-1989

부산지원 (우)606-080 부산광역시 영도구 동삼1동 522-1번지
TEL:(051) 403-7077   FAX:(051) 403-1077

울산지원 (우)683-500 울산광역시 북구 천곡동 927-7
TEL:(052) 295-2335   FAX:(052) 295-2336

제주지원 (우)690-140 제주도 제주시 영평동 1500
TEL:(064) 727-3100 FAX:(064) 727-0302

중부경남 (우)621-802 경상남도 김해시 진영읍 하계로 35번지
TEL:(055) 345-9900 FAX:(055) 346-2179

진주지원 (우)660-941 경상남도 진주시 미천면 오방로 528-40번지
TEL:(055) 746-8163 FAX:(055) 746-7825

청주지원 (우)360-814 충청북도 청주시 상당구 우암동 295-7
TEL:(043) 259-5599 FAX:(043) 255-5599

통영지원 (우)650-110 경상남도 통영시 도천동 113-3
TEL:(055) 643-0643 FAX:(055) 643-0642

포항지원 (우)791-220 경상북도 포항시 북구 우현동 13-1
TEL:(054) 232-3163 FAX:(054) 241-3503

Anyang Headquarters of Hanmaum Seonwon

(430-040) 101-62 Seoksu-dong, Manan-gu, Anyang-si
Gyeonggi-do, Republic of Korea
Tel: (82-31) 470-3175 / Fax: (82-31) 470-3209
www.hanmaum.org/eng
onemind@hanmaum.org

Overseas Branches of Hanmaum Seonwon

ARGENTINA
Buenos Aires
Miró 1575, CABA, C1406CVE, Rep. Argentina
Tel: (54-11) 4921-9286 / Fax: (54-11) 4921-9286
www.hanmaum.org.ar

Tucumán
Av. Aconquija 5250, El Corte, Yerba Buena,
Tucumán, T4107CHN, Rep. Argentina
Tel: (54-381) 425-1400
www.hanmaumtuc.org

BRASIL
São Paulo
R. Newton Prado 540, Bom Retiro
Sao Paulo, C.P 01127-000, Brasil
Tel: (55-11) 3337-5291
www.hanmaumbr.org

CANADA
Toronto
20 Mobile Dr., North York, Ontario M4A 1H9, Canada
Tel: (1-416) 750-7943 / Fax: (1-416) 981-7815
www.hanmaumcanada.org

GERMANY
Kaarst
Broicherdorf Str. 102, 41564 Kaarst, Germany
Tel: (49-2131) 969551 / Fax: (49-2131) 969552
www.hanmaum-zen.de

THAILAND
Bangkok
86-1 soi 4 Ekkamai Sukhumvit 63
Bangkok, Thailand
Tel: 070-8258-2391 / (66-2)391-0091
home.hanmaum.org/bangkok

USA
Chicago
7852 N. Lincoln Ave., Skokie, IL 60077, USA
Tel: (1-847) 674-0811 / Fax: (1-847) 674-0811
www.buddhapia.com/hmu/chi/

Los Angeles
1905 S. Victoria Ave., L.A., CA 90016, USA
Tel: (1-323) 766-1316
home.hanmaum.org/la

New York
144-39, 32 Ave., Flushing, NY 11354, USA
Tel: (1-718) 460-2019 / Fax: (1-718) 939-3974
www.juingong.org

Washington D.C.
7807 Trammel Rd., Annandale, VA 22003, USA
Tel: (1-703) 560-5166 / Fax: (1-703) 560-5566
http://home.hanmaum.org/wa

책에 관한 문의나 주문을 하실 분들은
아래의 연락처로 알려주십시오.

한마음국제문화원/한마음출판사
경기도 안양시 만안구 석수동 101-60
전화: (82-31) 470-3175
팩스: (82-31) 470-3209
e-mail: onemind@hanmaum.org

If you would like more information about these books or
would like to order copies of them,
please call or write to:

Hanmaum International Culture Institute
Hanmaum Publications
101-60, Seoksu-dong, Manan-gu, Anyang-si
Gyeonggi-do, 430-040, Republic of Korea
Tel: (82-31) 470-3175
Fax: (82-31) 470-3209
e-mail: onemind@hanmaum.org